1

The Earth was very cold.

3

A long time ago Australia was colder.

5

The Port Philip Bay was dry land.

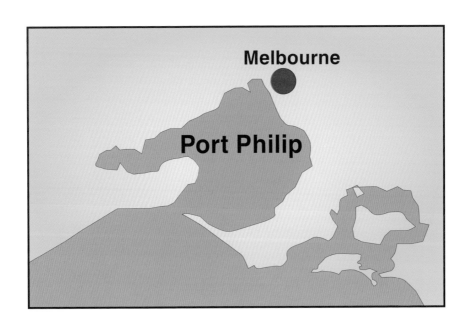

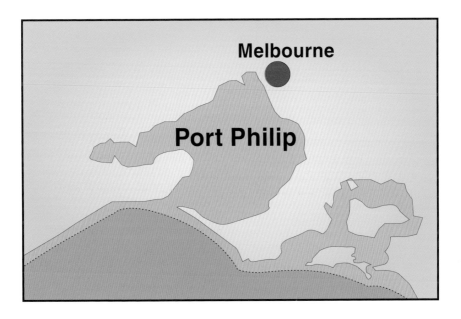

7

People could walk to Tasmania.
The sea was lower.

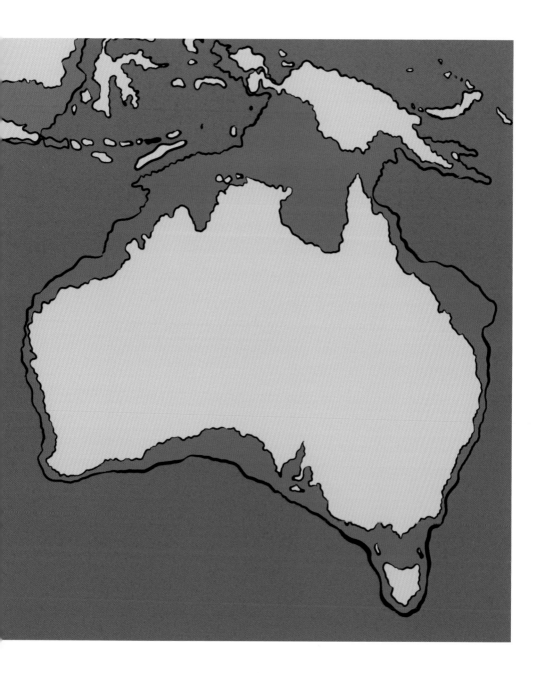

9

The Earth started to change.
The Sun was getting warmer.

11

The land and water were getting warmer.

13

The people saw a great flood.

15

There was more sunshine. The land got warm. The plants grew faster.

17

There was more water as the
sea got higher.

19

There was more food to eat.

20

21

Grass grew fast. It was warm now. There was more food for animals.

23

Word bank

grass

getting

fast

warmer

grew

water

animals

flood

food

Earth

cold

mountains

land

people

walk

Tasmania

down